World Series Champions: Los Angeles Dodgers

Pitcher Sandy Koufax

Outfielder Matt Kemp

WORLD SERIES CHAMPIONS

LOS ANGELES DODGERS

MEGAN COOLEY PETERSON

CREATIVE SPORTS

CREATIVE EDUCATION / CREATIVE PAPERBACKS

Published by Creative Education and Creative Paperbacks
P.O. Box 227, Mankato, Minnesota 56002
Creative Education and Creative Paperbacks are imprints of
The Creative Company
www.thecreativecompany.us

Art Direction by Tom Morgan
Book production by Ciara Beitlich
Edited by Joe Tischler

Photographs by AP Images (Doug Pizac, Marcio Jose Sanchez, Kevin
Terrell), Corbis (B Bennett, Cal Sport Media), Getty (Bettmann,
Sean M. Haffey, Hulton Archive, Jim McIsaac, MediaNews Group/
Pasadena Star-News, Maxx Wolfson), Shutterstock (Marek Masik)

Library of Congress Cataloging-in-Publication Data
Names: Peterson, Megan Cooley, author.
Title: Los Angeles Dodgers / Megan Cooley Peterson.
Description: Mankato, MN : Creative Education and Creative
   Paperbacks, 2024. | Series: Creative sports: world series champions
   | Includes index. | Audience: Ages 7-10 | Audience: Grades 2-3 |
   Summary: Elementary-level text and engaging sports photos
   highlight the Los Angeles Dodgers' MLB World Series wins and
   losses, plus sensational players associated with the professional
   baseball team such as Clayton Kershaw."-- Provided by publisher.
Identifiers: LCCN 2023008191 (print) | LCCN 2023008192 (ebook)
   | ISBN 9781640268265 (library binding) | ISBN 9781682773765
   (paperback) | ISBN 9781640009967 (pdf)
Subjects: LCSH: Los Angeles Dodgers (Baseball team)-History--
   Juvenile literature. | World Series (Baseball)--History--Juvenile
   literature.
Classification: LCC GV875.L6 P47 2024 (print) | LCC GV875.L6 (ebook) |
   DDC 796.357/640979494--dc23/eng/20230330
LC record available at https://lccn.loc.gov/2023008191
LC ebook record available at https://lccn.loc.gov/2023008192

Printed in China

2020 World Series Champions

Pitcher Clayton Kershaw

CONTENTS

Home of the Dodgers

Los Angeles, California, sits on the Pacific Coast. The Dodgers baseball team plays its home games there. Players and fans enjoy the sun shining down on Dodger **Stadium**.

The Los Angeles Dodgers are a Major League Baseball (MLB) team. They compete in the National League (NL) West Division. Their **rivals** are the San Francisco Giants. All MLB teams want to win the World Series and become champions. The Dodgers have done so seven times!

Outfielder Mookie Betts

Naming the Dodgers

The Dodgers first played in Brooklyn, New York. At that time, **trolley cars** ran through the city. People had to dodge them to cross the street. The team was called the Brooklyn Trolley Dodgers. The name was later shortened to Dodgers. The team had other nicknames before Dodgers. Among them were Robins, Atlantics, and Superbas.

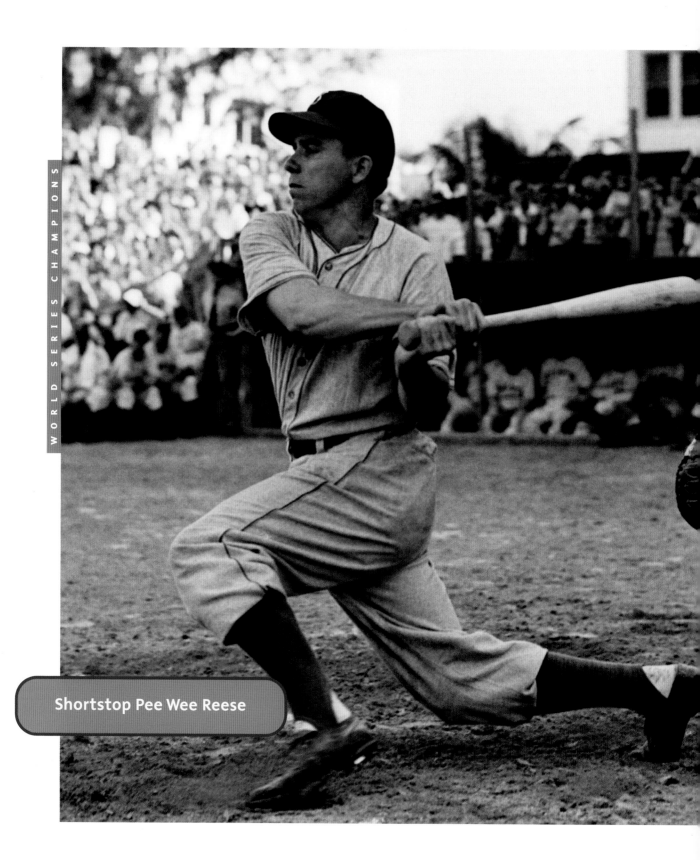

Shortstop Pee Wee Reese

Dodgers History

he Dodgers began in 1884. They joined the NL in 1890. In 1916, they appeared in their first World Series. They lost to the Boston Red Sox. They lost the 1920 World Series to the Cleveland Indians.

The Dodgers returned to the World Series three times in the 1940s. Shortstop Pee Wee Reese led the team. But they lost every one.

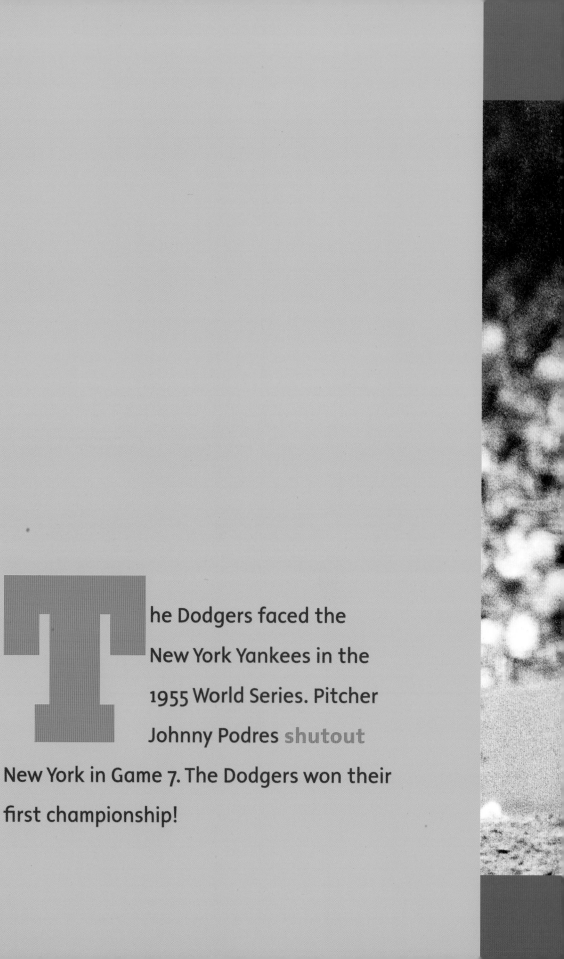

The Dodgers faced the New York Yankees in the 1955 World Series. Pitcher Johnny Podres shutout New York in Game 7. The Dodgers won their first championship!

Pitcher Johnny Podres

Shortstop Corey Seager

The Dodgers moved to Los Angeles in 1958. They won the World Series again in 1959, 1963, 1965, and 1981. They won their sixth championship in 1988. An injured Kirk Gibson hit a game-winning home run in Game 1.

The Dodgers returned to the World Series in 2017 and 2018. But they lost both series. They faced the Tampa Bay Rays in 2020. Mookie Betts and Corey Seager each hit two home runs. Pitcher Clayton Kershaw struck out batters. The Dodgers were champs again!

Other Dodgers Stars

Many of MLB's best players have been Dodgers. The team signed star second baseman Jackie Robinson in 1947. He was the first Black player in MLB history. Sandy Koufax was one of the best pitchers in baseball. He used his curveball to win 165 games. Great pitching continued with Fernando Valenzuela in the 1980s. He thrilled fans with his **screwballs**.

Second baseman Jackie Robinson

First baseman Freddie Freeman

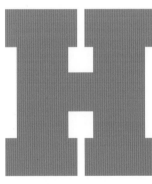all of Fame catcher Mike Piazza started his career with the Dodgers. He was named NL Rookie of the Year. He also played in five-straight All-Star Games. First baseman Freddie Freeman is one of baseball's best hitters. Fans hope the Dodgers will add another championship soon!

About the Dodgers

Started playing: 1884

. . . .

League/division: National
	League, West Division

. . . .

Team colors: blue and white

. . . .

Home stadium: Dodger Stadium

. . . .

WORLD SERIES CHAMPIONSHIPS:

   1955, 4 games to 3 over New York Yankees

. . . .

   1959, 4 games to 2 over Chicago White Sox

. . . .

   1963, 4 games to 0 over New York Yankees

. . . .

   1965, 4 games to 3 over Minnesota Twins

. . . .

   1981, 4 games to 2 over New York Yankees

. . . .

   1988, 4 games to 1 over Oakland Athletics

. . . .

   2020, 4 games to 2 over Tampa Bay Rays

. . . .

Los Angeles Dodgers website:
	www.mlb.com/dodgers

. . . .

Glossary

rival—a team that plays extra hard against another team

screwball—a pitch that makes the ball move in a direction that the batter does not expect

shutout—to pitch a complete game without allowing the other team to score

stadium—a building with tiers of seats for spectators

trolley car—a passenger vehicle powered by electricity from an overhead cable

Catcher Mike Piazza

Index